HAWK MOON

A BOOK OF SHORT
STORIES, POEMS
AND MONOLOGUES
SAM SHEPARD

1973
BLACK SPARROW PRESS
Los Angeles

LIBRARY OF CONGRESS CATALOGING IN PUBLICATION DATA

Shepard, Sam, 1943—
    Hawk moon.

    1.   Title.
PS3569.H394H3   1973   813'.5'4   72-13808
ISBN 0-87685-145-6
ISBN 0-87685-144-8 (pbk)

for
Patti Lee

TABLE OF CONTENTS

HAWK MOON

*"A boy has never wept nor
dashed a thousand kim."*

—*Dutch Schultz*

HAWK MOON MONTH

Hawk Moon month November month my birthday month month
of cold set in month when secrets start whisper on the mesa high old
ancient sacred land of Hopi month Antelope deer and antler clan
first signs of barren empty need for prayer first dance snake in
mouth dance spirit dance snake mouth painted hand and lightning
bolt month of washing long black hair my month of birth month—
the Hawk Moon month.

BACK IN THE 1970's

The kids prayed for a pool hall, fought hard on Friday nights right in the middle of the highway, stopping traffic. No knives, guns or chains. Just fists. Nobody was after blood. Not like city fights. The dances at Diligent River always drew a big crowd and big fights broke out between rival towns, just like back in El Monte Legion Stadium days. Boredom was the big killer. No jobs, no pool hall, ten guys to one girl and that one was usually ugly, bad radio stations, old people dying and drunk, church bazaars, one dance a month and not even Rock and Roll, one juke box that never changed its records, heavy cold snowbound winters and foggy summers. The most exciting thing that ever happened was somebody shooting a moose or a bear and that was pretty rare. Then the Americans came. First a little trickle then a whole river. Draft dodgers, criminals, escapees from the cities that were blowing up right and left. Strange pornographic literature began to circulate through the villages. Full-blown color pages of cock and pussy and tits and ass. Drugs seeped in like salty sea air. Rock and Roll hummed and blasted out of the forests drowning out the chain saws. Teepees and strangely shaped domes with glaring colors and weird designs. Long flowing ribbon banners fluttered in the fields amazing the crows. Black and chrome monster motorcycles chomped into the dirt lumber roads. Stampedes of choppers and hogs roaring through fishing villages. Rolling Stones posters pasted to the sides of barns and churches. Tattoos showing up on local girls in places you'd never think of. The Mounties were called in but things were too far gone. There was no way of telling a Canadian kid from an American. Everybody fucking and sucking and smoking and shooting and dancing right out in the open. And far off you could hear the sound of America cracking open and crashing into the sea.

THE PHANTOM TRAILER

A phantom trailer moves through the back lawns. It's been taken over by leather bandits, Mexican whores and dogs. Before that it was owned by an old couple who bought it and moved to the desert for their lungs. Now they lie without their heads in a Death Valley ditch. The driver pulls the trailer with a '56 Chevy ½ ton painted steel blue from what it used to be. He lost one eye on the horn of a six point buck while he was trying to skin it alive. He sings in Spanish and speaks in tongues when the radio goes on the blink. In the bed of the truck is a Blue Tick Coon Hound named Jude tied by rags which she chews but can't get through 'cause she's too old and lost her teeth on buffalo bones. A little girl from Quaxaca feeds Jude with Antelope meat that she chews on for hours for the juice then spits the pulp in Jude's mouth. Inside the trailer the color T.V. is the center of attraction and everyone crowds around it in a half moon shape. Because it's never been turned off day or night the sound doesn't work and the color's been distorted to bright green. Only two channels work and they both show the news but the people don't seem to care. There's one old man named Felix who never watches the news but just walks in a perfect square hugging the walls of the trailer and crossing himself with a picture of Kennedy all faded and torn in his left hand. They stop sometimes on the outskirts of town and shoot one golden spider web flare into the sky to let the High School boys know they're there. We watch from our windows on the seventh of every other month and when we see the signal we all go down in pairs, dressed in tight peggered pants and white bucks and tight T-shirts with our Camels rolled up in the shirt sleeves. We wait in the woods by the drainage ditch and sit in our '32 Fords blinking the lights on and off. Felix comes out with a flashlight and blinks us back. Then we fight for who goes first. The fights are always silent and fast because nobody wants to shoot their whole load. The losers go last but sometimes wind up the best 'cause by that time the girls are so tired that they even come and call out our names. I always got the feeling that they liked the losers

13

the best. Once me and a girl named Lupe (who was the skinniest) even came at the very same time. Just once that happened and I'll never forget. The next time the trailer came around she was gone. They told me she died in San Diego when some guy put Spanish fly in her Coke and left her in his car to go get a rubber. When he came she had the stick shift shoved so far into her womb that she bled to death.

CLAW CLOUD

He was so fat he couldn't get down off the tractor. The old John Deere just sat there popping and hissing in the green sun. The harrow stood ready, waiting with its claws to grab into the earth. There was nothing left to do. The potatoes, the corn, the beans, the peas. Not a weed in sight. Sweat ran down into the grease and crackled on the steel. He turned the key off and the engine cranked down to a halt. Wind from the north hit him across the chops. He just sat there looking in four directions then finally to the little speck of a white house in the distance. He thought he saw a beautiful tall blonde woman come out the front door and wave for him to come in for dinner. But she vanished. Then he saw a yellow flag with a green maple leaf raise itself slowly on the flag pole and burn itself up when it hit the top. There was a cloud directly above him in the shape of a bear claw. The only claw in the sky. The only cloud. A shiver went through him but he didn't shake. It wasn't cold. He wasn't scared. Just fat and tired. He wanted to move his arms and legs. The impulse was there but nothing happened. Ducks flew in a "V." Dust rolled the smaller rocks. He looked down at his fat hands gripping the wheel like clamps as though he were still plowing. He felt the blood roaring to the surface. Something began to happen. He was turning to stone. Slowly. As hard as a rock. In his feet and hands then moving up until his whole body was petrified. He couldn't move a finger. Rooted in the earth. The claw cloud came down and scooped him up with one sweep. He rose into the air light as a ribbon. Rolled and danced and tumbled like a weed. His mouth opened wide and the wind gushed in like water. He let loose an animal sound like a great Black Bear and the whole earth shuddered. The tractor fell on its side with the front wheel spinning. The house far below snapped open its doors and the windows burst their frames. The crops uprooted and flew up like crows. By this time tomorrow he was far out over the ocean causing a tidal wave. Small ships pointed up at a strange fat black claw cloud in the sky and prayed.

BLOOD MILK

The spirit goat moved white with its long goatee and pointed horns, tied by a chain, in a circle, going in a circle, the same circle path, well worn with shit and piss by hooves. All this under a spotlight from the tar paper shack. Bugs, moths, mosquitos clumping in buzzing bunches, cracking into the glass, falling and rising in vertical lines all around the light and head of the man sitting on wooden planks with a captain's cap whittling a ship with a jacknife. She'd milked right through the winter without being bred, over a quart and a half a day. But lately the milk had started getting a pink tinge to it and in the mornings blood settled to the bottom of the bottle. The Captain didn't mind though. Once a cow he'd milked for three years straight did the same thing and the blood went away. He drank it right along. It reminded him of a strawberry milk shake. Each day the goat milk had been getting pinker though until finally it was bright red and about two thirds blood to one third milk. He kept drinking it just the same. He said it was good for the eyes. He noticed the change in the goat's pupils from day to night. How in the day the pupil narrowed down to a black horizontal slit in a yellow eye to keep out the sun's rays and at night the pupil opened all the way to let in more light. His were doing the same. He could feel it. He liked that. He liked getting close to animals that way. Learning their tricks. Feeling their souls. The goat would dance sometimes and play with the flying chips of wood that sprung from the knife. He'd talk and sing to her and cluck like a chicken. She'd baa back and a language began to set itself up. Pretty soon he'd baa three times and she'd do the same. Then she'd baa a certain number and he'd answer. Between the two creatures baaing a third voice made itself heard. They both listened. It told them to look to Venus. So they did. A light flashed and exploded in the sky but they weren't afraid. The voice came again: "Do you know where you are?" Then disappeared. They couldn't answer. And the next day the milk turned white as snow.

16

SLEEPING AT THE WHEEL

"Let's face it, we know very little about the total picture and that's the truth." His piss burned a whole through the thick wet pine needles. I stood around watching then took one myself, feeling a little awkward about watching. We climbed back in the old Plymouth. I was set to go but he sat there fiddling with the keys and remarking about the Redwoods. "Fuck analyzing. I mean who's the analyzer. Who's the judge. Who's the big one. There's too many in there working at once. All clanging around with their hands raised, trying to get a turn." "Right," I said. "Like this car is going to look like a prairie schooner to people fifty years from now. Say you came from another planet and landed here for a visit. Just to check things out. Where would you go first?" Not realizing this was a direct question I stared out the cracked window at a kid in a tree house throwing pine cones at a black dog. "Where would you go. Well you sure as hell wouldn't go to the back woods or some little fishing village. You'd head straight for the Big Apple. Times Square, 42nd Street. That's where you could really study the planet earth."

"Maybe we should get back to the girls," I said sort of half assed. It seemed to work though. He slid the key in and turned her over. We rumbled off, down the mountain. "I mean every once in a while I'm just amazed when I catch a glimpse of who I really am. Just a little flash like the gesture of my hand in a conversation and WHAM there's my old man. Right there, living inside me like a worm in the wood. And I ask myself 'Where have I been all this time? Why was I blind. Sleeping. Just the same as being asleep. We're all asleep. Being awake is too hard.' " This set me to thinking of a story that a friend of mine from Saskatchewan once told while we were driving North on Route 96. I asked him if he'd ever been in a bad car crash and he laughed like it was some kind of joke. He said he used to get in one every week. The worst one he said was when he was driving back from someplace where he'd been drinking for two days and nights straight without any sleep. It was night

17

time and he kept falling asleep at the wheel and shaking himself awake, slapping his face and pinching his leg till it bled. The next morning he woke up and found himself still in the car at the wheel. He opened the door to get out and put one foot out but couldn't find the ground. He looked down and saw that his car was stuck in the top of a huge oak tree about thirty feet off the ground. He looked up and saw where he'd smashed through the barricades off a bridge and people were lining up to take a look at the accident. Finally he just climbed down out of the tree, waved at the people and left the car there to rot.

"I mean where have we been all this time. What happens between the past and the future."

"You got me," I said and settled back, pretending to be asleep.

HORSE THIEVES

Horse thieves in dark black to match the day hands and knees
through crawdad brook horsefly grass brush silent signals split and
circle old corral with pinto black and bay heads down munching
oats switching blue blow flies closing in sliding up like old friends
touch blankets flanks twitch wild eyes head up jerks and circles
once then stops takes hackamore rope bit in teeth bites loose then
both swing up and jump clear running wild out straight for blue
space rifles blazing tongues amazed at wind and free strong power
headlong into who knows where.

DAKOTA

Outside Rapid City flat blue grey Sioux plains a sign with a light old red peeled paint says see the last of the great buffalo in sawdust broken pails and crumbling corral the cow and her calf in half moon light touched by the hand of one old man says he knew Kit Carson back when he'd shoot an Injun or two for breakfast the cow snorts flying sawdust chips the calf sucks the cars drone past going too fast to stop for a sideshow.

MONTANA

He sat there on the bed counting his money. Five thousand in cash. Mostly hundred dollar bills. He began licking one side of the bills and pasting them with a vacant feeling on the tits of the naked corpse. He started feeling better already and covered the whole body with the bills. He'd always wanted to be a sculptor. After the girl's body was completely covered he got up and walked to one side of the room and squinted his eyes halfway like his mother taught him and took a long look at his handiwork. He moved to different parts of the room and did the same thing. He chuckled but caught himself. He walked to a desk, pulled open a drawer and drew out an old Buntline Special with an extra long barrel. He handled the gun and ran his fingers along the smooth black barrel and spun the chamber twice. He put the gun to his head and pulled the trigger. CLICK! He spun the chamber twice again and went to the girl's body. He spread her legs and slowly pushed the barrel up into her womb. He pulled the trigger again. CLICK! He withdrew the gun and spun the chamber, aimed it at the head of an owl statue and blew it apart. The bullet hit the plaster wall with a thud. He fell on the floor laughing. He struggled to gain control of himself. Now was no time to go off the deep end. He finally stopped his hysterical laughter and lay very still staring up at the ceiling. He began to very slowly put himself through some Yoga positions. He'd been noticing how his flow of blood was slowing down. First he did the Plow for about five minutes. Then the Cobra. Then a head stand. Then the Lion. Then a few breathing exercises. After this he began to feel the blood flowing freely and felt refreshed again. He got up off the floor, shook himself like a dog and walked to the closet. He opened it and pulled out his favorite cowboy gear: Kangaroo skin boots in white with red flower designs and a high riding heel. Big rawhide chaps with fringe and silver Navajo studs. A black satin Gene Autry shirt with white pistols embroidered on the collar and cuffs. His favorite bright orange Roy Rogers bandana. His Lone Ranger mask. And a black stetson hat with a chin

21

string. Finally he pulled out the golden spurs with silver chains and leather straps. He laid them all out on the floor in the right order so they looked like the shape of a man. The Super Cowboy Man. Then he took off all his clothes and walked naked to the window of the hotel. He opened the French window and walked out onto the terrace. The wind hit him cold but the sun was still out. He stared up Twenty-third Street to the East River and the Con Ed chimneys with their red rings around the top. Then down Twenty-third to the Hudson. He breathed the wind and looked down seven stories at the little people then across to the Y.M.C.A. where the Indians were having a pow-wow. His legs were getting goose bumps so he jumped back inside and closed the window. He stopped and looked again at the naked body covered with money. Then at the cowboy shape on the floor. He walked over and picked up the shirt and put it on. Then the chaps. Then the boots. Then the spurs. Then the bandana. Then the hat. Then the mask. He stood up and walked to the mirror. He picked up the gun and did a few twirling and fast draw tricks then stuck the barrel inside the waist of his chaps. He was well pleased with what he saw. Now what? He'd like to go down to the bar for a drink. A Scotch and soda or a bourbon or something. First he should turn on some music so the neighbors wouldn't know he was out. He picked out the *Sticky Fingers* album and put it on the stereo full volume then left the room. He could still hear *Wild Horses* all the way down the elevator. It gave him a good feeling. Like someone was taking care of her while he was gone. He got to the bar and sat down next to a man who'd had his voice larynx thing removed so he had to talk through a plastic tube which made him sound like a transistor radio. The baseball game was on and the Spanish waiters were complaining about the Espresso machine and how the steam burned them all the time. He watched the game for a while but baseball always bored him. Stock car racing was his favorite sport aside from the rodeo. He turned to the man with the voice box and asked him if he knew anything about cremation. The man was a little shocked by the mask and the question but said something about pouring gasoline over the body

22

very lightly in order to save all the ashes. So he finished his double tequila, paid the bill and went outside for a cab. He headed straight for "Joe's Friendly Service" in the Village. His favorite gas station because it was so old and run by a Swede who loved New York. He asked Joe for a gallon of super octane in a can and left a deposit then hopped back in a cab and drove back to the hotel. All the way up the elevator he could hear *Moonlight Mile* coming loud and clear from his room. He walked in and there she was, still covered with the money, still sleeping forever. He set down the can of gas, walked to the bed and lifted her up and carried her into the bathroom. Hundred dollar bills floated to the floor and fell from her tits. He set her down softly in the cold bathtub with most of the money still clinging to her skin. He opened the can of gas and sprinkled it lightly along her legs, over her waist and chest and head and hair. Then he bent down slowly and kissed her on the lips. The taste of gas in his mouth made him feel like hitting the road. He struck a match and tossed it on the body. The bills burst into flame and then caught her skin. Her body went up like a torch. The skin crackled and popped and turned black under the bright orange rage. The body twisted from the heat and turned to one side. He could almost see her eyes through the flaming licks. He stood there cold and empty for a long time until the fire died and smoke rose in little curls. Then he turned the shower on and watched the ashes spin down the drain leaving nothing but bones and teeth on the white porcelain. He shut the shower off, pulled the curtain and walked back into the room. He picked up four hundred dollar bills off the floor and stuck them in his shirt pocket. He put the needle on *Sister Morphine* and walked out the door leaving it wide open. All the way down the elevator he could hear the song. He went straight through the lobby, threw his key on the desk and walked out to hail a cab. A big yellow Checker drew up. He swung in with his spurs jangling and said: "Montana please."

23

HEAVEN'S FIST

Far shooting star
Scar branded night
Car light snakes a trail
On earth
Far far heaven's head
Opens up its bony skull
Shows a flash of secret sight
Then fast the fist slams shut

LONG TALL SALLY

Cool and weary
Tongue tied down
Back strapped to a wind mill
Round and round
Long Tall Sally
In the alley
Caught and taken
For a witch

SPIRIT

Spirit
With a wet nose
Lump on the neck
Sits in corners of my room
Says not to fear
Breaks the windows to breathe
Then leaves
Like that

STRANGER

I keep waking up in whoever's
Body I was last with
Who's this
Arms like a Viking
Rolled bull muscles
Hair down to here
I'm enough of a stranger as it is

I couldn't believe I was all alone. Puking lobster into a bucket and carrying it outside in the dark. Dumping it where the fox would probably find it. Carrying it back in and trying to sleep. Knowing there were ghosts. Hearing the fog horn. Watching the night swallows bashing into the window. Praying for morning and sun and happy thoughts. What a night. I remember a prayer that went: "Great human wild animals. Keep watch over them." And I started to talk it then sing it to myself, then out loud to the blackness. I kept up the chant, doing it first in Soul rhythms, then Calypso, then Country Western then Rolling Stones then waltz time then back to Soul. As I did this I opened a Moose Head beer and guzzled and paced the house. Whenever I got the urge to vomit I'd sing the prayer harder and louder and almost angry against the demon. I couldn't make out his shape but I knew him from a long time ago. His face was grey and long. He kept wanting me to change the song, to change the rhythms, to pick up knives and slash myself but I kept away. I sang the prayer in his face. I'd sweat and tremble when he touched me. I never begged. I fought. I bit his finger off and spit it down the stairs. He screamed and pushed me after it. I hit the floor and rolled. I rolled with every punch, protecting my kidneys and groin. I sang as I rolled. I crawled into the kitchen and lay face down on the floor. He changed his shape to small crawling things of the dust and skittered across my back making pin hole teeth marks in my neck. "Great human wild animals! Keep watch over them! Keep watch over them!" He pulled me out onto the porch by my arms and kicked at my head. I ran to the alders and hid. I could hear him coming like a snake. I ran for the open fields but fell and lay still in the cooch grass. The moon moved faster than the clouds. The race was on. I pulled myself up and got to a gulley where the marsh began. He was on me again. Slashing at my back. I slid to the bottom and sank in putrid smelling water. I covered myself in the stuff and half swam the best I could. Like a dog sinking in a lake. He gurgled behind. I sang at the night. The spring peepers

28

answered me and made me strong. Strong enough to win. I made it to the beach and ran straight into the ocean up to my waist and stopped. The freezing water brought me to my senses. This was the test. To go straight ahead and never come back or to turn back now. I stayed like that until morning singing my song. When the sun came the bottom half of me was frozen stiff, the top half was warm.

GUADALUPE IN THE PROMISED LAND

Guadalupe hit the skids and fishtailed into a ditch, crawled out of the wreck bleeding from the neck, saw the moon, laid his head in a mud puddle, said "Todo el Mundo" three times and snuffed out. Him and Manolete got together after that and Manolete told him it wasn't enough just to be a man. The thing to shoot for was sainthood. He said he almost hit it. A saint of the cape. Jackson Pollock joined them and told Manolete he was full of shit. A man was good enough. That was harder than sainthood. There's too many saints anyway. Guadalupe didn't know what to think. He ran into Jimmy Dean and Jimmy just looked confused. Marilyn Monroe had no opinion. Brecht kept talking about Germany and shame. Satchmo kept wiping his sweat and shuffling. Janis wanted more. Crazy Horse said: "Fight and die young." Brian Jones just played the harpoon. Dylan Thomas said "Rage." Jimi Hendricks said "Slide." Bip Bopper said "What?" Johnny Ace said "Shoot." And Davey Moore said "Take it all on." That made sense to Guadalupe. And with that he lay down for a nice long rest.

DESERTED

Fangs out it lunged for meat and cracked its head on the glass. Fell back, belly up in a tropical miniature garden. Like a nine hole pitch and putt minus the pitchers. Squirming, flopping over, right side up and panting, sides heaving, scales swelling and falling, cracking off like paint. Begins to move and slide in a sideways shuffle through the moss and fern and finds a white mouse, swallows it whole like a fly and keeps on going. Avoids a giant pink fingered tentacle hand with bitten-off nails and axle grease and black and blue thumb. Runs right into another one and silently screams, slashes with teeth and claws but is caught firm around the midriff and hoisted like a plane over six feet in the air. Then set down suddenly and left in a giant open-air arena with no glass forever and stars for lights and moon for more. Miles and miles of this going on and on. The sound of the tentacled one's car fading off in the distance. Can't move. Frozen with vastness and uncertainty. The silent boom of desert. Deserted. Left to be wild and not knowing how anymore. Not needing to be. It slowly eats its tail and hind legs and belly and swallows itself whole. In the morning a truck roars by without a driver, the radio blaring. Just the truck, the radio and the desert.

WIPE OUT

(To be read while listening to Wild Horses)

After playing *Wipe Out* all day and all night for three full days
without stopping even to snort some coke or rest his calluses, Cobra
Moonstar fell on top of his Les Paul Gibson and broke his nose. He
didn't care. It felt good. More good honest pain. The little Fender
Princeton amp buzzed and sputtered like a '32 Ford, the tubes
flickering golden light like the morning coming up. Cobra's stomach growled like feedback. The garbage trucks were starting up
their crunching grinding. Cobra thought of Dylan's *New Morning*
and knew what it "meant." He let out a long fart that smelled like
"Good and Plenty" since that's all he'd been eating before he went
on his fast. He wished he had a woman around to make a coke run
or massage his back or give him some head or just talk about something like early Yardbirds or just rub his head or something. He
couldn't feel his fingers. His ears were buzzing, throbbing with electric waves. The floor felt good. The guitar was a little uncomfort-
able as a pillow but nothing mattered like that. His animal spirit
was king. He'd cracked through. Now he had his chops. Now he'd
earned his half moon tattoo on his left hand and his pierced ear.
The blood from his nose was forming a little river. He watched it
run across the floor heading straight for his collection of old forty-
fives. He licked it and lapped it up like a puppy. Nice and salty.
The crab lice he'd picked up from a *Vogue* model he'd balled twice
last week were starting to wake up in their pubic nest. He didn't
care. It tickled a little but he was too tired to scratch. Their movement was even kind of exciting. Like friends saying good morning.
Friendly. He felt his balls moving around, shifting position. His
joint started swelling. He remembered how embarrassed he used to
get when he was a kid and he'd get a hard-on from petting his dog.
Trying to hide the bulge in his crotch. Digging around in his pock-
ets and shifting the position of his cock so it stood straight
up and laid flat against his belly. Now he didn't care. He laughed

at his old self like it was another person. His joint grew hard and strong now and reached out for food like a baby bird's neck. How come now when he was so tired and wasted? He could call up Sheila or Mabelline but he didn't really want to fuck. An orgasm would be nice but not all the love making preparation, undress "do you love me?" stuff. Just to come would be nice. "You can't always get what you want," he thought candidly. The guitar sure felt good now. He licked the Super Slinkies and remembered Jimi Hendricks in the old days. He licked some more on the strings surprised at the similarity in taste of the steel to the taste of pussy. His tongue ran up and down. Maybe it was the combination of blood and steel. Like bleeding pussy. Nice. Even the smell. His joint was throbbing now. Blood rushing. Even a tingle like the real thing. He tried to fantasize a beautiful chick like Brigitte Bardot or Anna Karina or Tuesday Weld but they didn't seem to matter. The Gibson was good enough. She was turning the trick. He unzipped and yanked it out rubbing it between the volume knobs. With each stroke his cock made the Gibson howled. The volume knob rolling with the strokes. This was really something. He was really getting it on. The guitar seemed to dig it too. The harder he pumped the more she screamed. The more she screamed the harder he pumped. He ripped at the strings with his teeth. The E string snapped and whipped across his face. His tongue ran up and down the neck getting at all the frets. His hands reached out for the amp and caught hold. Just as he came a bolt of electric shock struck through him like lightning. His hands turned blue. His hair jumped out straight and turned white. He screamed with the Gibson and came all over her. Long stringy white lumps of rushing come gushing and gushing like boiling over pudding. His whole body went stiff, taut like a bow. Then it was over. He fell limp and rolled over on his back panting and gasping for air. He just lay there staring up at the ceiling for a long time. Then he laughed. "If you try sometimes you can get what you need," he thought matter-of-factly.

SILENT STAMPEDE

Night moss marsh in moose in flesh grass marsh wet strings of reeds and hooves in mud track beach track tractor track sound of chain saw ripping bark rip tree rip moose run herds and herds stampede the white village through the church bloody priest antler gash and rip down store and walls all hell breaks loose the Eskimo Ice Age old age old age weather summer fall spring ice break ice breaker North shake earth shake day shake night shake star shake day break light and sound off pole off bounce and splinter quakes and shifts the poles earth axis earth hemispheres and balls and spheres and globes and knots and nuts and bolts hold together holding holding screws and nuts break holds bust loose off balance tip and twist turn ripping sideways shifting Moon for Venus turn and turn the secret Venus turn hand Venus secret silent secret silent turning Moon Venus silent secret silent secret Earth.

CAN A ½ TON FLY?

Green Moon scraped the cow shit off his boots and bent down to smell it, stuck his finger in it, wiped it off on his shirt tail, shuffled to the stove and threw a log on, knocked over a pint of whiskey and growled, got down and licked it up, pulled a splinter out of his tongue and punched his fist through the side of the cardboard shack. He stood there drunk and dazed with his arm half inside and half outside. He felt the difference in the weather outside and in. Then he punched his other fist through and felt what that was like. Same thing. When Skunk Tails arrived in the ½ ton Green Moon was still like that, both his hands and half his arms sticking through. Skunk Tails grabbed a piece of rope from the bed of the truck and snuck up on the hands. He quickly grabbed Green Moon's arms and pulled them tight then wrapped the rope around both wrists and tied a square knot so there was no escape. Skunk Tails giggled and went back to the truck, hauled out a six pack and some bourbon and went into the shack. Green Moon was unconscious on the floor with his arms still stuck up in the wall. He looked like a slaughtered lamb. Skunk Tails giggled some more, opened a can of beer and poured it over Green Moon's head. That brought him around but he couldn't figure out how come his arms were stuck through the wall. Skunk Tails giggled and Green Moon let out a bellow like a bull moose and pulled half the wall of the shack down. He lay on the floor with his hands still tied. The hole in the wall let in the cool night and you could see all the lights down in Yellow Knife. Green Moon was really pissed off by this time because Skunk Tails just sat there and giggled, guzzling beer and slapping his knee. Green Moon rolled around on the floor, crashing into the stove, biting at his wrists and pounding his head on the floor. Finally Skunk Tails stood up, took out his jacknife and cut him loose. Green Moon tackled him to the floor, grabbed the knife away and slashed Skunk Tails across the knee. Skunk Tails just laughed and poured bourbon all over the wound. Then Green Moon laughed and took a long pull on the bottle. They both sat there on the floor staring out the hole in the wall at the lights reflecting off the water. They decided to go down and pick up their friend Fox Hand and take a drive through the town. Fox Hand was busy frying Caribou eyes but he left them burning and joined his friends. They drove for a while through every street and alleyway in Yellow Knife, singing and pounding on the dashboard. Green Moon went unconscious again. The town was dead and buried. Fox Hand suggested they go across the draw bridge and look at the lights from the other side of the river.

On the other side of the river was a car full of tourists waiting patiently for a ship to pass under the bridge. The iron tongues of the draw bridge began to rise slowly up into the sky. The bell was ringing and red lights blinked on and off. The ship slowly slid its way up to the slot. The tourists watched an old grey ½ ton pull up on the other side and stop. One of them said: "Those look like Indians." Another one said: "Could be, or Eskimos maybe." Then they watched the ½ ton start up again and move half way up the rising bridge. One of the tourists gasped and clutched a hand to her chest. "They must be crazy!" But the ½ ton stopped again. The ship moved closer and nudged its nose into the opening. The ½ ton started up again and moved straight up to the top of the rising tongue and plunged straight off into thin air. The tourists screamed as they watched the truck smash against the bow of the ship and plunge into the river sending up huge green gurgling bubbles. The ship went on, the draw bridge closed and the car full of tourists drove back to where they came from.

SEVEN IS A NUMBER IN MAGIC

Seven nurses still dressed in white standing on a cement island in the night with yellow flashing lights causing cars to skirt the island, out late after a night on the town and drunk laughing, telling jokes about the handsome doctor, the ugly old man with the leaking bladder, the psychosomatic lady with serum hepatitis and the cars picking up their skirts and wolf whistles aimed at their legs, without fear of any danger in the air, just the city fun of being young and free after working hours.

Seven twelve year old kids riding beat up customized Schwinns and stolen bikes with racoon tails flying from the handle bars and raised up seats and little wheels in front and big ones in the back and high risers and mud flaps with red and orange reflectors and the Ace of Spades stuck in their spokes come riding up and form a circle around the seven nurses closing in and making sounds of cats in heat. At first the nurses laugh and make "oh brother!" faces at each other then they try to move on down the street to a place with more light and more people walking by. But the kids close the circle in and start to wave silver car antennas like whips in their faces and call out Spanish names which the nurses catch the meaning of. Now the panic starts and the nurses cry out for what they want and the kids say to dump their purses out in the middle of the island. The first one says no and gets a slash across the face with the silver whip. She screams and gets another slash. One of the smart ones dumps her purse first and the others follow suit until a big mound of lipstick, wallets, perfume, tissues, Tampax, coins and bills, stamps, hairpins, false fingernails and polish, hair spray, pictures of lovers, powder puffs, and files lie strewn across the pavement. The kids ride through it with their bikes, crushing and smashing all the stuff and grabbing handfulls of money with their teeth the way cowboys do at the rodeo. The stupid nurse who screamed tries to make a run for it across the street and one of the kids with "El Corason" written across the back of his purple silk jacket rides after her, doing wheel stands and burning rubber right on her heels.

She falls like a calf and the kid leaps off his bike, pulls a switch-blade and cuts off her left ear. He turns and raises it high to his comrades, dripping with blood and stuck on the tip of the knife. They call out "Ole!" and ride off with the kid with the ear in the lead.

The next day the six nurses bring the seventh one with one ear a transistor radio to her room in the hospital where she used to work. They all make jokes about at least she knows what she's in for.

The kid with the nurse's ear sits on top of a roof on his haunches staring down at the ear. He drives a hole through the white lobe with a nail and threads it on a leather thong then puts it around his neck. He stands up and raises a fist to the sky. The Gods are well pleased.

WHO WOULD'VE THOUGHT

Who would've thought the English would cop our music. Who would've thought our music would cop the world. Who would've thought Africa would cop America. Who would've thought the Indians would cop the French. Who would've thought Brecht would cop Dylan's mind. Who would've thought that time was on our side.

HOLLYWOOD

The cowboy dressed in fringe with buckskin gloves, silk bandana, pale clown white make up, lipstick, eyes thickly made up and a ten gallon hat, holds the reins of his horse decked out in silver studs. The cowboy squints under hot spotlights. The gaffers all giggle. The cowboy sweats but there's nowhere for the sweat to go. He sinks to his knees and screams: "Forgive me Utah! Forgive me!"

GUAM

A jeep bounces violently through lush jungle green hanging wet dripping plants with snakes. The mother fires four shots from her revolver out the window through the thick rain, the kid on the floor in a cowboy hat covering his ears. The Japs run for cover in loin cloths and sneakers, one bleeding from the side, and hide in caves. The jeep crashes on through to black sticky asphalt and the ride smoothes out. She sticks the gun back under the seat and pats the kid on the head. They arrive at the drive-in theatre and stop, plug in the speaker and sit back to watch *Song of the South.*

Down in the sweat pit. The leaders have told me to stay until my vision comes. I sweat it out for days. "I'm not a visionary!" I keep screaming. Bashing my head with stones. The old men come in once a day and pour cold water on the hot stones then leave the place looking like L.A. on the worst smoggy day. I hack my way through the steam to the bolted door and call out for "at least a cheeseburger!" but they're long gone. My stomach jumps like a frog. "How can torture bring you peace! I'm just a dish washer, not a warrior!" They already have plans for my marriage to the ugliest girl on the block. My uncle Buzz is giving her father six black Ford Mustangs and a Castro Convertible for the deal. The trouble is I used to like her when we first moved in but now I can't stand the publicity. I keep waiting for a sign but nothing comes but sweat and hunger. Not even imagination. I go over and over the possibilities in my head: "I'll go along with the whole thing. Play dumb. Marry the chick and go on our honeymoon. Then I'll ditch her. But then they'd send their best scouts and find me. Bring me back and humiliate me in front of the whole block. Maybe even make me do the Sun Dance. I couldn't stand that. The pain. More pain! I can't stand the pain. No. I'll die like a man. I'll lie and tell the old men that I've finally had a vision. They'll let me out and take me to the Moon Dreamer. Then I'll tell him I lied and that I don't wanna marry that stupid girl. Then they'd kill me. They'd stone me to death like the Tasavuh." There's too much at stake. There's too much confusion in here. And I'm the only one. How can that be. There must be some way out. I've tried digging but the place is surrounded by Malamutes and Huskies. I wouldn't stand a snowball's chance in hell of making it to the woods without being ripped apart. If I could only dissappear. If I could just sweat myself away. That's it! If I concentrate I could probably do it. I could probably just turn myself into a pool of sweat on the floor. The old men would come in and I'd be gone. A miracle they'd say. They'd celebrate the day each year by having drag races and roping off the main streets. Block dances and parties and Mardi Gras parades in honor of a Saint. A Sweat Saint. Firework displays and rodeos and ox pulls and dog races and art shows and costume balls and swimming meets and footballgames. All for me and my memory. But now the pit is getting muddy. The clay walls are cracking from the heat. My skin and the walls. My sweat and the mud. My breath and the steam. My head and the stones. My bones are going soggy and outside the drums have already started up.

BLACK BEAR RUG

I keep seeing a black bear rug in front of my face
Wherever I go it stares back at me
In Horn and Hardardts
There it is
I see myself sitting before it on a wooden floor
Smoking a pipe
Eskimo still
Listening to the Huskies outside ripping into their fish
It doesn't speak
It wants nothing from me
It doesn't seem at all dead though
Even though it's just the skin and fur and head and claws
And beady black berry eyes
It seems pathetic and strong
It won't answer when I ask its name
I threaten it with a Bowie Knife and all it does is grin
I take it for walks in the moonlight and it just drags its ass
I take it fishing and hunting but it doesn't care
I try to fuck it from every angle
Give it head
Up the ass
It won't have any of it
So tonight I threw it in the fire
The stink was awful
All that's left is the claws
I wear them around my neck
I wear them wherever I go
I'm real lonely for that bear

DREAM BAND

Rattle. A plane flash. Baby whimper. The house moans. The droning plane. Birds play. My tattoo itching. Anne Waldman. New Jersey. Long Island. Michael's lungs. Black spot from the Midwest. Eddie Hicks. LouEllen. All their Babies. Miners in the cave shaft. Murray and his Cheyenne headband. His grey Mustang rusted out. Feet, hands. Lubricating sweat glands. The body's secret machine. Patti and the Chelsea. David making rhubarb wine. His new camera. Scott and Annie. Their black roof. Jeeps in four wheel drive. Sand and beach. Endless. Rattle. Wisdom teeth. Bleeding gum flap. Hydrogen Peroxide. The Beach Boys. Duarte High. John and Scarlet. Kristy and the old man who gave her presents. The Sierra Madre mountains. The Arizona border. Dylan in shades. The ship. The missile. Rattle.

THE CURSE OF THE RAVEN'S BLACK FEATHER

"Drive you fool. Up under the dashboard. Checkin' out the fuses. For a man who knows nothin' about cars but memorized the rear ends of every Chevy from 1950 to '59 you do pretty good. You're not in competition that's for sure."

You know the way a person can get in your head and stick there and roll around and you start to think about all his good points and then his bad ones and then just about him as a person? Well that's what I'm thinking about Keith Richard.

That's the thing about driving a distance, especially if you're alone. Driving alone is mainly just sitting and moving with the road. A stationary kind of act but the car keeps moving while you sit still and your feet fall asleep. Your mind races like the engine, a camera gone wild, but your body stays put. That's the thing about driving.

The thing about Keith is his shark tooth ear ring, his hawk face and his name. Not Richards but Richard. Keith Richard, two first names. "You got the silver, you got the gold. You got the diamonds from the mine." And he kicked some Scotch guy in the teeth from the stage in the early days when they played in Scotland before jeering crowds.

Some smell from the floor boards sneaks up on me like burning rubber then changes to sweet maple syrup smelling. It's funny 'cause when it smells like burning rubber I get worried and tense and wonder if we'll make it. When it changes to maple sugar I relax and feel real good about bein' back on the road. On the road, on the road, on the road.

A shooting pain through my stomach. Jack Kerouac died like that. French Canadian. I'm heading for Canada. Home of Jack.

His stomach burst and bled from lush. I haven't touched a drop in three days. Maybe I need a drink. Some Navy Rum. 151 proof. Enough to kill a horse.

"It's just about a moonlight mile down the road." Down the road, down the road, down the road.

Visions of wrecks. Visions of wrecked stars; Jayne Mansfield's severed head. Jackson Pollock. Jimmy Dean. Visions of wrecked cars. Asleep at the wheel. Shaking head. Broken line. Yellow line. Solid line. Solid white line. Broken white line. Broken bones. Broke down. Stranded. Hitching for gas. Hitching in the dark. Stranded. Headlight. Searchlight. Spotlight. Flashing light. Night light. The little glowing blue ember in the kid's room to keep away the Boogie Man. Carburetors, spark plugs, generators, regulators, internal combustion, power of steel. The iron horse. But that's a train.

KEITH standing alone, outside in the California night. Standing in his Python boots staring at a kidney shaped pool. The kind Brian died in. Staring at the water. The air blowing his crow feather hair.

A RAVEN! A dead black bird hit on the wing! I slam to a stop, jump out and pluck a long plume for luck. The corpse jumps from being plucked. I jump back in and shove the feather behind the sun visor. It sticks out black. I drive and think of a movie called *The Raven* where everybody in the movie keeps saying the stuffed Raven in the movie is a symbol of death. I wonder about that. I begin to wonder. Am I going to die? Is everything a sign? "Soft Shoulder." Is everything a sign? Is it bad luck to take a dead Raven's feather? Is it diseased? From the touch of the feather. Could I die from the touch? Could I crash? I slam to a stop and run down a steep bank to a brook of clear water and wash the hand that touched the feather. I watch the curse wash away. I'm clean again. I get back in but the feather's still there. I can't touch it again or the curse won't never

47

leave. I drive and drive like being chased. Running away.

DESTINATIONS: From some place to some place. But in between is where the action is.

The feather speaks! I'm sure of it. It has a voice. Its own peculiar voice. More like a Myna bird than a Raven. No, more like a "Nevermore" Edgar Poe Raven voice. It doesn't matter. The character is too distinct to describe. It has a voice. It definitely speaks to me. It speaks low and soft like a feather should. It mumbles with the pistons then stands out clear. Then shouts. Then lies quiet. I wait, thinking maybe I should rest. Maybe I should sleep in the back seat. Maybe it'll go away when the sun comes. Maybe. But no. The voice says this:

"Notice the way the moon beam shining on the water chases you. Chases you. As though you were the only one. No escape. I'm taking you to a special place."

"Me? Look, I'm sorry I took your feather but I thought you wouldn't mind. I mean you were dead and everything."

"My body on the asphalt. My claws. My feathers speak. My bones. My feathers speak."

"I know. Why is that? I can't figure that one out."

"It's not for you to figure. Just follow. I'll show you the way."

"But I have a date in Canada. I'm late already."

"I'll take you there then let you go."

"Where? Take me where?"

"South."

"But I'm heading North."

"Not anymore."

And sure enough the signs were reading "South 201" and "South 306" and South and South and South. And how was I to know what to believe. So I went along with it. I couldn't fight it anyway. Once I tried turning around and going the opposite direction but the signs still read "South" and "South" and "South." So I was going South against my will all on account of a feather. I began to realize that part of the problem was no radio. Not having a radio was probably causing me to hear things in the air that weren't even there. If only I had me a radio. So I stopped at a radio shop and bought one. A small black Panasonic. But all that came out was the voice of the Crow. The voice of the Raven's black feather urging me on. Softly flying me South.

"You'll take me to a town called Noir in Louisiana. You'll drive straight through the town to the outskirts where you'll find a dump. A car dump full of wrecked cars. You'll park and get out of your car and walk to an old black 1936 Pontiac sitting alone off to one side. You'll get in on the driver's side and open the glove compartment. Inside you'll find six black feathers just like mine. You'll put my feather in the glove compartment with the others and close it. Then get back in your car and you're on your way."

"That's all? That's all you want me to do?"

"That's all."

Keith and Mick. Like brothers. Like evil sisters in disguise. The left and right hand. A two-headed beast. The music and the words. The background and the foreground. The opposite of Paul and John. The dark and the light. I've always been pulled toward darkness. Toward black. Toward death. Toward the South. Good.

49

Now I'm heading the right direction. Away from the quaint North. Away from lobsters and white churches and Civil War graveyards and cracker barrel bazaars. Toward the swamps, the Bayou, the Cajuns, the cotton mouth, the Mardi Gras, the crocodile.

For days I went on like this. Never stopping. Driving day and night. But they seemed the same. The dialogue never stopping. And the car kept going. I never stopped for gas even. And the car kept going. And the Crow stopped talking. I even started asking it directions but it never answered. Just some friendly conversation but it never answered. Finally I hit a town named Noir in Lousiana. I wasn't surprised. I drove straight through to the car dump and stopped. I took the feather and got out and found the old Pontiac. I got in and opened the glove compartment and laid the feather down with the six other black feathers and closed the glove compartment door. I sat there for a while just frozen. Expecting more directions I guess. No answer. I looked through the cracked glass. Nothing. I played with the wheel for a while and diddled the gear shift. I looked down and there was an old rusted key in the ignition. Not thinking I reached down and turned the key. The old engine turned right over and barked. I wasn't surprised. I put her in reverse and backed up through the piles of smashed metal and glass then drove straight out onto the highway. Straight North. I've been driving for years like that. Just North. Always going North and getting no-where. Never stopping for gas or food or sleep or friendship. Just driving. North.

¼ MILE

Race pass blue on asphalt blue and orange lightning bolt of glass splintered cam shaft reeled and rimmed and hooked to the left and left in smoke and blue and blue and gone gone far asphalt ground to meat and steel and blue and blue and ground crowd cheer hook of cheer and plague of cheer of ask for more and more and ground in glass smash of steel cold and blue and blue and chants of more of more of bulls of blue of bulls of ground of ground in blood of flood of wave of drown of rave of rage of rave of cave of seat of crash helmet strapped in blue lightning rod of orange and blue like Rams in blue and crash and crash and leather smash on smash on smash on and on.

MILE AND A ¼

Hoof and turf class horse flash and green and lean and little jockey seat hot walker trot and gate flash steel gate bell ring ring car off-track betting with Italian gangster mobster ring in blood in barber shop where Anastasia got his flash steel stirrup cold bet in the pari mutuals the killing was made for gold for gold for silver gold and python boots and hookers toots and Cadillac waits and sits and tracks sleep sleep in hay and mangers dogs and circles of smoke camp talk of Derby Louisville the Downs down leather strapped to horse flesh smell of horse hair sweat and fetlock hoof and bit and bridle chomp and bell rings bell the gate of Hell opens to the dirt fresh harrowed by the mule team skinners from your South where black wears black and numbers in your paper Herald paper numbers fill your Times and gold and silver slivers clang and clang and chime to church where the mobsters pray for St. Jude saint saints a saints day parade a bullet through the back and dead and bang goes the colt from California on his setting pace bang again he come from comes from bay black and bay tan and black mane tail and doesn't know little does he know the murder outside the mile and a quarter.

MR. AND MRS. SIZZLER

A yellow and green balsa wood glider like an old Russian Mig hangs by a rubber band from a holly bush under Christmas lights by the front porch of a home in the Hollywood Hills. It weaves and bobs, springing like, on the rubber band from a gentle breeze. Night's just coming in. The smog's lifting. Out back the smell of T-bone steaks sizzling over open coals with the fat dripping down and popping. White German Shepherds play—fight and roll down the long green rolling lawn bumping their heads on rain birds and yipping. Dark tan kids toss a yellow and black plastic ball back and forth in the heated pool with underwater lights shining through the pale blue chlorined water and a dead moth floating near the drain. The father stands staring into the barbecue with a long fork in one hand and wearing a long white apron with the words "Mr. Sizzler" printed in red across the front. A big Boeing 747 flies over low with yellow and blue lights flashing, heading toward the L.A. Airport. "Mr. Sizzler" looks up and remembers World War II. "Mrs. Sizzler" comes out of sliding glass doors, walks across the flagstone patio with her arms folded across her chest and a cashmere sweater thrown over her shoulders. They both stand there silently staring into the red coals. Just the sound of the kids and the dogs and splashes in the pool. Then BLAM! the house blows up.

BOREDOM

Boredom was on. For dinner they ate the porkypine and shot the shit and rattled through the license plate collection, telling a different story for each state. Arkansas: "How the bear almost got Hodie." Wyoming: "The different ways they fold their hats." Mississippi: "The mongoloid idiot with the mud skiff." Two of them went off with a gallon of white gas to blow up the beach. Two more drew a circle on the wall and threw fishing knives. Two examined Venus and talked about the Hopi prophecy. The seventh stared at the mouse shit and wished for a gun. Any gun. A blue gun. A fast gun. A slow gun. A gun fight. A good fast gun fight. A Winchester, lever action 30.30. Now there's a gun to take care of anything. They look good too. Make you feel good to hold one. Like a cowboy again. Somebody was asking him to wash the dishes. He got up and broke the chair over their back. Somebody else wanted to know why he did that. He said he was dreaming of guns.

RIP IT UP

Drum bass the ghost pedal sizzle ride cymbal top hat old dixieland New Orleans way of putting it driving a band of hill billies
into rock hard rock soul rhythm and blues a fight between the lead
guitar and the piano player for volume the guitar wins natch the
inside workings of a band the audience never sees the constant difference between the inside and the out the performer and the per-
formance the experience and what they experience Rock and Roll is
definitely a motherfucker and always will be Rock and Roll made
movies theatre books painting and art go out the window none of it
stands a chance against The Who The Stones and old Yardbirds
Credence Traffic The Velvet Underground Janis and Jimi and on
and on the constant frustration of the other artists to keep up to the
music of our time Rock and Roll will never die but what about the
novel the theatre and all that culture stuff Norman Mailer insisting
on being a man Edward Albee working from dawn to dusk for
Broadway Peter Townsend says Rock and Roll is the perfect medium
for self destruction and he don't mean suicide Joe Cocker said if he
hadn't started singing he probably would have killed somebody
what other art can come close to that the dancer trapped in form the
actor trapped by the script Rock and Roll gets it on better than football baseball even boxing because how many knockouts or knock-
downs or T.K.O's. do you see in a fight one if you're lucky and even
then it's usually down on one knee every time I saw The Who in the
early days it was like watching Sonny Liston hit the canvas from
start to finish the whole place going up in smoke Rock and Roll is
violence manifest without hurting no one except an occassional kick
in the teeth or punch in the mouth Rock and Roll is more revolution-
ary than revolution fuck James Taylor and all them sweethearts of
the guitar pick ballad school gimmee hard ass shit kickin' music
like *Hey Joe* and *Down Home Girl* and *Summertime Blues* the way
The Who did it Chuck Berry's *School Days* Little Richard Otis and
Booker T. and Jerry Lee ROCK AND ROLL ROCK AND ROLL
ROCK AND ROLL ROCK AND ROLL ROCK AND ROLL "We're
gonna rock it up we're gonna rip it up and ball tonight."

55

ANGEL AND THE CROW BAIT

The motion animal breaks down
A little at a time
Broken horse time
Gelding with swollen fetlocks
Hoof rot from standing in the marsh grass too many days
The winged animal begins to swing in lower circles
Not looking for prey
Just praying not to crash
In Science talk it's called entropy
In Whiskey talk the shakes
In Dope talk the turkey
In Murder the heart
In Poker the bluff
In Mexico the shits
Out here we don't speak its name
We know it by the look in the fire
Angel feeds on Mule Meat and don't think about the body
He buries himself to sleep
I have to dig him out every morning
By night the dust leaves him shining
Venus combs him clean
To disappear he smears his nose in charcoal and drops
his ear ring in the frying pan
I save it for him
We meet up in a Gallup Pawn Shop
He trades the ring for an Eagle claw on a leather thong
He makes me pierce his nose with a hot toothpick
The claw hangs down over his black teeth
He's happy now
To celebrate we steal a jukebox and take it down to the dump
It plays all night on good faith
A red Coyote wants to dance but Angel scares him off with
the claw

And I'm getting slower all the time
And night don't catch me yawning
Just staring
Just stunned
Starving
And day don't catch me running
Just amazed at the way they used to spell "Ford"

AND SO DOES YOUR MOTHER

I'm tired of this Pop Star Sentimental
Reminiscing on old '40 Fords
And the Beach Boys
And wasn't the Fifties neat
The Fifties sucked dogs man
And so do you
And so does your mother too

ANOTHER TONIGHT

You wake me up with your pale body
And your snake scar
I dreamed of the Great White Shark
And you of tattoos of crashing planes
On the cheek of a Cuban lady
I have to meet a faggot for lunch
But I'll be back for another tonight

LEFT HANDED KACHINA

In Old Oraibi on the high mesa in Arizona, the oldest settlement in the Western Hemisphere, a Buick pulls up, a tourist and his wife get out and go into a small broken down store and ask about rugs. Old Hopi women with grey braided hair sit around weaving, looking up once then eyes back down. Wikvaya ("one who brings"), a young Hopi, comes into the store and stands in a corner staring at the tourists making them nervous enough to leave. Wikvaya follows them outside and approaches them before they reach the car. He asks them if they want to buy a Kachina doll. They hadn't thought about Kachinas, what they mainly wanted was a rug, but at this point any souvenir of the trip would be good enough. The tourists get in their car expecting to follow Wikvaya in his but instead Wikvaya gets in the front seat right along with them. This is pretty scary for the tourists and exciting at the same time. A real live Indian riding in their car. Wikvaya points out the way and they follow his instructions. Down through small tar paper shacks and huts along a bumpy dirt road. The man would like to carry on some bit of conversation but can't think of anything to say. The woman is concentrating on keeping her right leg from touching Wikvaya's left leg. Wikvaya could care less about any of it. He just stares out at the village with night black eyes. The road twists and turns until it looks like there's no more houses in sight and the man begins to panic. "What if he's taken us out here to murder us? He probably hates white people. After all you can't blame him. All those years of oppression." Then the road runs right up to a small shack with smoke coming out a piece of rusty pipe with wire holding it to the roof. Wikvaya gets out and walks up to the shack. The tourists follow. Conversation in strange broken language mixed with English comes from inside. Wikvaya opens the door and silence falls as the tourists enter the one room. Several young Hopis, some in crew cuts and glasses, one with a transistor radio, one reading an Archie comic book, sit in chairs and on the floor all around the sides of the shack with their backs up against the walls. Corn husks hang

60

from the beams and rafters and one large table filled with Kachina dolls of every size and color and type. A few of the Hopis are whittling softly with jackknives on half-finished Kachinas, looking down, eyes not touching the tourists. Wikvaya explains what they've come for and one of them motions to the table. Wikvaya tells the tourists to take their pick. They go to the table and pick up the first one that strikes their eye, anxious to get the hell out of there. They hold up a white one with green stripes. The Hopis shake their heads no, explaining that it's not finished. They hold up another and the same thing happens. Finally they find a black and red one with a bow in the right hand and a rattle in the left. This one they say they can have for fifteen bucks. That seemed a little steep to the tourists but they pay it anyway, not wanting to get into an argument. They say thank you and good bye to Wikvaya then leave with the Kachina tucked under an arm.

Back in New York City the man sets his Kachina on the bookshelf and looks up what type it is in a pamphlet he bought in Phoenix. According to the picture he finds it's called a Left Handed Kachina but nothing tells about what it represents or what it's for except probably to make rain. He goes out and buys a twenty dollar record of ancient Hopi chants recorded by the National Archives in the early nineteen hundreds, brings it home and puts it on the record player. He sits back in his easy chair staring proudly at the Kachina and listening to the ancient drum beat and moaning throb of voices from another time. The Kachina doll suddenly pitches forward off the bookcase, lands on the floor and breaks both arms. The man rushes over and picks it up. His hands begin to sweat. The right hand getting cold and the left one hot. He thinks nothing of it, his big concern is fixing the doll. He finds some epoxy and applies it to the wood, puts the arms back in place and wraps rubber bands around them to hold them firm. He sets the doll back on the bookcase to dry and puts the record back on. By this time he begins to notice his hands more and wipes the sweat off on his pants leg. He closes his eyes and leans back in the chair letting the chant roll over him in waves. In the blackness he sees a long coiling green snake with a horn in its forehead come sliding straight toward him, fangs out and head weaving from side to side. Again the doll falls from the bookcase, both arms snapping loose and sliding across the floor. The man sits straight up, eyes open, fear creeping in. The chant pounds on over and over shifting rhythm and tone. He jumps to his feet and takes the needle off the record but the chant keeps on. He goes to the doll and tries to glue the arms on again but his hands are trembling, sweating. The arms slide from the body to the floor. His right hand is freezing cold, the left hand boiling and the heat creeping all the way up his arm very slow like rattlesnake venom. He finds a rag and makes a tourniquet at the left elbow but his right hand is so cold that the rag keeps slipping from his grip. He pulls at the rag with his teeth then bites down into the veins of his arm. He lets out a low animal moan and finds his voice making the chant. He moves like a dog around the apartment moaning and chanting slashing at his arm. The blood leaves snaking red trails across the carpet. Rain pours from the ceiling soaking, driving hard like needles into his face. Thunder cracks the plaster and lightning slashes through the furniture burning black brands across the walls and floor. Corn springs from the carpet. Rivers gush and spread red earth into all the corners of the apartment. His wife opens the door with an arm load of groceries, accidentally steps on the Kachina and smashes it to bits. Everything stops still. She looks down at the doll then at her husband weeping, moaning, swaying back and forth in a tight ball in the middle of the floor. She drops her load.

RHYTHM

If everything could be sung to the standard rock and roll progres-
sion—C, A minor, F, G chords—then everything'd be simple. How
many variations on a single theme. The greatest drum solo I ever
heard was made by a loose flap of a tarpaulin on top of my car hitting the wind at eighty. The second best is windshield wipers in the
rain, but more abstract, less animal. Like the rhythms of a rabbit
scratching his chin. Vision rhythms are neat like hawk swoops and
swan dives. Slow motion space rhythms. Digging rhythms like shov-
els and spades and hoes and rakes and snowplow rhythms. Jack-
hammer rhythms make Ginger Baker and Keith Moon look like
punk chumps. Oilcan rhythms, ratchet wrench rhythms. Playing
cards in bicycle spokes. A string of rapid-fire, firecracker rhythms.
Propeller rhythms. Cricket rhythms. Dog claws clicking on hard-
wood floors. Clocks. Piston rhythms. Dripping faucets. Tin hitting
tin in the wind. Water slapping rocks. Flesh slapping flesh. Boxing
rhythms. Racing rhythms. Rushing brooks. Radio static buzz in a
car when the engine is the dictator. Directional turnsignal blinkers.
Off and on neon lights. Blinking yellow arrows. Water pumps.
Refrigerator hums. Thermostatic-controlled heating systems.
Clicking elevators with the numbers lighting up for each floor.
Snakes sliding through grass. In fact any animal through grass.
At night. Buoy lights. Ship signals. Airplane warnings. Fire
alarms. Rhythms in a stuck car horn. Eating rhythms. Chewing
rhythms. The cud of a cow. The chomp of a horse. Knives being
sharpened. Band saws. Skill saws. Hack saws. Buzz saws. Buck
saws. Chain saws. Any saw rhythm. Hammers and nails. Money
clanking in a poker game. Cards shuffled. Bus meters. Taxi meters.
Boiling water rhythms. Clicking ballpoint pens. Clicking metal
frogs. Roulette wheel spinning rhythms. Tire rhythms. Whittling.
Stitching. Typing. Clicking knitting needles. Parrots sharpening
their beaks on wood. Chickens scratching. Dogs digging for moles.
Birds cleaning their feathers. Cocking guns. Spinning guns. Bolt
actions. Lever actions. Snapping finger nails. Finger popping.

Cracking knuckles. Snapping bones. Farting. Spitting. Shitting. Fucking rhythms. Blinking eyes. Blowing nose. Coughing without control. Candle flicker rhythms. Creaking houses. Thawing ice. And you call yourself a drummer?

PEACOCK KILLER

My dog caught a peacock one night and ate it. The next day when I found out I kicked the shit out of him. I broke three of his ribs and cried. Then I found out how dumb peacocks are even though everyone thinks they're beautiful. Shitting on your roof and screaming when they fuck. So I bought a twenty-two and started killing every peacock I could lay my hands on. Me and my dog at night we'd go hunting. I had to use short bullets with a mushroom head so they wouldn't make too much noise. Just like the sound of a small car backfire. Just one shot apiece and if that didn't kill 'em I'd let my dog finish them off. We'd come home bloody and laughing with murder every night. In the mornings the rich neighbors would wake up and find the corpses chewed and blasted up against white picket fences. They hired a private detective to investigate the deaths. Soon it hit the local papers: MAD PEACOCK KILLER ON THE LOOSE. So I changed my tactics. I switched to bow and arrow. I marked each arrow with a special notch and attached a note which read: REVENGE FOR BROKEN RIBS.

LETTER FROM A COLD KILLER

Maybe you'd love me more if I didn't kill for a living
Having to smell my Luger Blackhawk every night
Counting the bullets like my pay check
It's true we move around a lot and it's hard on the kid
You get used to the Dodge and the next day it's gone
At least he gets to see the lay of the land
He loves the trains and the passport changes
What's a lie now and then
The blood on the tie
He's seen that in the movies
Pass it off for lipstick
The powder burned eye
Tell him the matches exploded
Or better yet tell him I'm a Cold Killer
Trying to pay his way through College
And give him a kiss on the head
And tuck him in his bed
And write down what he mumbles in his sky blue sleep

SHARK MOVE

The way a shark can't stop moving or he'll die
That's you on the floor
Sleep swimming on your back
Spitting out your teeth
Sliding like a puck
I can't do nothin' for you 'less you stand up
What you need is a pocket full of crickets
To bring you back to earth

ILLINOIS

Illinois green lush wet dripping corn bacon and tomatoes the size of your fist fights across the table brother fights father and wife fights father son fights sister brother fights the priest makes his visit interrupts the ball game sits down for a meal demanded just on account of his collar upstairs Jesus bleeds from different positions on the walls crosses nailed to rafters beams and plaster old radios dixieland drums echo across the barn the Springer Spaniel has her litter wet and licking milk from straw old hats and halters paper clippings Truman Roosevelt Churchill trucks rumble the bridge milk trucks gasoline and apple brandy for the old man wet wooden porch screen watch the wind go by neighbors picking up mail crows strut flap leave black feathers on the lawn gravel sing of high electric wire baseballs rotting in the leaves bats broke and mitts rubber gloves wires growing through trees and Grandpa dies in his slippers and Grandpa dies in his baseball cap and Grandpa dies sitting up.

INSTANT ANIMAL

He was talkin' about the imagery in a good fight
I didn't get it
An outsider no doubt
Him I mean
Talkin' about this guy spilling hot coffee on this other guy
And the good time it was
No stitches
No hospital
No emergency
Just a good yuck
He was talkin' about trust
Measured by action in a life and death move
If someone's there or not there
To be present at death
At the same time in the same place
I'll always trust a dumb guy before a smart one
An instant animal
With no thinking gaps
The gap that kills
The watcher watching the watched
An outsider no doubt
Me I mean

POWER

I can remember racing with my father
The difference in our size and strength
The power in his legs
The quickness in mine
It almost killed him but he won
And afterwards I heard him puke behind the shed
That night I went to bed
And dreamed of power in a train

"CITY OF HOPE"

On the outskirts of Duarte, California, it's dry, flat, cracked and stripped down. Rock quarries and gravel pits. Trucks roll from sun to sun. People in the outlying towns call it "Rock Town." "The Ctiy of Hope," an institute dedicated to curing and investigating the causes of cancer, sits there surrounded by rocks and cement companies. It provides most of the town with work of one kind or another. Famous doctors and medical men from all over the world come to visit and catch up on the latest discoveries. A lot of experimenting is done on animals. All kinds of animals from mice to rats to hamsters to dogs. They're all injected or fed cancer-causing bacteria and then slowly die and are then operated on by the famous doctors and then the bodies are burned in huge incinerators. The smoke and stink of death hangs over Duarte most of the time. A kid named Jaimie Lee takes care of the experimental greyhounds. They're kept in a special kennel house separated from the main building, out in the middle of an open lot. He arrives each morning at 6:30 sharp in his '51 Chevy, puts on a long white apron and rubber gloves and boots and gets down to work. There's over twenty-five purebred greyhounds all raised and brought in from Arizona. As soon as one dies there's a new one to take his place the next day. Jaimie has to shift the dogs from their dirty kennels over into clean ones. Then he hoses down the shit and piss and vomit into a gutter. Sometimes on dogs specially marked with yellow or red collars he has to save the shit in a dixie cup and put it in a small ice box for the Japanese doctor to examine later. Then he feeds and waters all the dogs except for certain other specially marked ones who are going to be killed and operated on that day. If he finds a dead dog in the morning he's supposed to call the main office and notify the doctor in charge then wrap the dog in a plastic sheet and place him in a large freezer. Jaimie gets to know each dog personally as they come in and makes up names for them since all they have is numbers when they come. After two or three weeks they start to respond to him like a friend. As soon as they hear his car roll up in the morning,

71

all twenty-five dogs start barking their heads off. He walks down the cement aisle and talks to each one and gives them each a pat on the head. He notices how thin and bony they get after the first week or so and how sleek and healthy they looked when they first came. In the afternoon the doctors come around to give them their injection of poison. There's one favorite dog that Jaimie has that he calls "Swaps." He called him that because one day he let Swaps out for a run in the vacant lot and he couldn't believe how fast and beautiful he was. So he named him after his favorite race horse. It was Swaps' coloring that first attracted Jaimie. A deep red and black brindle color, like a tiger. He found out that Swaps came from a breeder in Arizona who had raised him especially for racing but the dog grew too big so he was shipped to "The City of Hope." Jaimie knew that if he ever got caught letting any of the dogs out for a run that he'd get fired. But he didn't care. Swaps loved to run and Jaimie loved to watch him. He'd always come back when Jaimie whistled and go right into his kennel. Whenever Jaimie took Swaps out all the other dogs would go crazy, barking and howling and throwing themselves against the cyclone fence. On this particular morning Jaimie had finished all the dirty work and went to get Swaps. He swung the gate open and Swaps danced and leaped all around Jaimie and headed straight for the door of the kennel house wagging his tail with joy. Jaimie opened the door and Swaps bolted out like a bullet straight into the morning sunlight. He ran in great circles at top speed, gravel and dirt spitting out from his paws. Jaimie stood in the doorway and watched. What a beautiful wild animal. It got so that Jaimie's vision could slow Swap's movement down to slow motion like a camera. He could see every muscle move through the shoulders, along the ribs, down through the back legs. The power in every pull and leap. The beautiful tiger stripes flashing across the earth. He wished Swaps would just keep running and never stop, never come back to die. He started to think about Swaps being dead. He saw visions of his corpse in the morning. How he'd have to wrap him up and put him in the freezer. How the Japanese doctor would cut him open with precision and indifference

72

and examine his insides. How he'd have to burn the mutilated body afterwards. The other dogs were barking louder now from inside. Louder than usual it seemed. Every bark nagging at him. Tugging at him. Pulling, demanding. Screaming out for room to run. He turned back inside and looked down the dreary grey cement hallway with the dim electric light bulbs. He went to the first kennel and unlocked it, swung the gate open and a dog he'd named Silky bolted out, went through the open door and blasted into the morning. He went to the next one and opened it. Another one sprung loose and another. On down the whole aisle until all the cages were empty. Just Jaimie Lee standing there alone inside with the smell of wet cement in his nose. He went outside and there was Swaps standing big and regal. The leader of the pack. The rest of them swarming and dancing around him. Jaimie took off his apron, his gloves and his boots and threw them in the dirt. Swaps was watching Jaimie's movements from a distance. Jaimie got in his car and took off down the road. Swaps was hot on his heels with the rest of the pack following along behind. Jaimie looked in his rear view mirror and saw the twenty-five greyhounds stretching out along the highway. He was pacing them at forty miles an hour and they were keeping up. He smiled and turned a right into the main gates with "City of Hope" written in giant letters across the top. Smooth green freshly mowed lawns and immaculately clean white buildings. Nurses wheeling patients in wheel chairs came to a screeching halt to watch the procession. The dogs tore across the lawns, through the corridors, breaking away from the pack then joining it again. Swaps kept the lead the whole time, trying to catch Jaimie's car. Doctors stood open mouthed, some running for cover. Then Jaimie hung a left and headed up the road toward the Safeway Shopping Center. Then he hit the Bank, the Post Office, the Library and the Park. The dogs never seemed to tire. They couldn't get enough of it. He headed straight out toward Azusa. Then Cucamunga and Upland and the grape vineyards. It was there he lost them. All except for Swaps whom he kept for a friend.

YOUR JUICE

Wicked
Tasty
Red
And ripe
To touch
To have
In hand
The juice
Of you

MOON PRAYER

Sacred
Night
Moon
Sacred
Light
New
Like a man
Precious
Time
Precious
Few
Worship the animal
The animal
You

ARSON

You have to go on your belly for a long way, then half standing, then crawling on all fours under alders, then walking up to your knees almost in standing algae water that smells like rotten wood. Sometimes you can skirt the impossible passages by going up the shaggy sides of the mountain and around the spruce trees watching out for dead porkypines 'cause they still got their quills and if you get stuck by one they just work their way in deeper and deeper. Finally you get to a place where different kinds of sycamores grow. Don't ask me how they got in the same place with spruce and alders, but they're there. The area up there opens out more and there's room to move around in. You start collecting dry twigs, sunburned leaves and the shaggy bark from the sycamore. Birch bark is best. Then you build all these up in a pile in a dry brushy place close to dead trees and small bushes and in the open enough to catch the wind. Then take a long book of paper matches like the kind they give out in fancy hotels and tie a long piece of white string soaked in kerosent to the match book. Place the book of matches in the middle of the pile of kindling and light the string, then run. Find an open fire path back that runs in the opposite direction of the wind. Once you get down the mountain find a high tree well covered with leaves and climb it. Sit there all night and watch the beautiful orange glow eat up the blackness and listen to the far away snapping and booms as trees explode and fall like planes shot down and smell the blue smoke cut through the mountain air and pinch at your nose like a starving man cut off from a barbecue.

THE SEX OF FISHES

They were talking about the corniness of the word "slice." Then she said an even cornier one was "portion." What kind of people use the word "portion"? Then that got 'em laughing for a while. They were waiting for company. In the mean time he loaded up the .22 with longs and went out to squeeze off some crows. Five times he missed but they left the garden alone after that. The goat didn't like the shots too much and began dancing on her hind legs, her udder slapping from side to side. As he took the bolt out of the gun and set it in the cupboard he was thinking of his mother. How she was coming to visit and probably make comments on the length of the baby's hair. "Boy or girl? Boy or girl?" He looked at his woman as he re-loaded the clip with five more shells. She looked like a little boy doing the dishes. His hands looked long and slender like a woman's. The gun looked male through and through. The deer were female, even the bucks. Porcupines, little fat boys. Ducks—chicks. Moose—men. Fox—female. Wolves—a little of both. Rabbit—girl fuzzies. Fish? He couldn't place. A fish is a hard one to place. Fish are definitely mysterious. With that he packed it in for the night.

SEA SLEEP

The bed was an ocean to him even when he was awake. The blankets swirled like the waves. The sheets crashed like the white caps. Seagulls dove down and fished along his back. He hadn't been up for days and the people in the house were getting worried. He wouldn't talk or eat. Just sleep and wake and fall asleep again. When they called the doctor he pissed all over him. When they called a psychiatrist he spit. When they called a priest he puked. Finally they let him be and just slid carrots and lettuce under the door. These were the only things he'd eat. The people in the house started a joke about their pet rabbit and he overheard it. His hearing was getting very keen. So he stopped eating altogether. He slid the bed in front of the door so no one could get in and then fell fast asleep. At night the people would hear hurricane sounds coming from the room. Thunder and lightning and foghorns. They banged on the door. They tried to break it down but the door held firm. They put their ears to the door and heard gurgling underwater sounds. Moss and barnacles started to grow on the outside walls of the room. The people were afraid. They decided to have him committed but when they went to get their car they discovered the house surrounded by ocean on all sides as far as they could see. Nothing but ocean. The house tossed and heaved all night. The people huddled together in the basement. From up in the room came a long low moan and the whole house sank into the sea.

CLEAN GREEN

Seventy-five fathoms
Down
Six feet to the fathom
Six miles
Out
Drunk to a rip tide
Snared by a rock rope
Dragged to the deep blue
Bottom
Bones unseen
Just the clean green table top
Waiting for the next pool shark
To come play fish

SNAKE TIDE

Snake tide
Sneaky
Green
Foam break
Slips up
Back
And soaks the dry
Thirsty earth's
Cracked cry
Of longing to be out there
Moving
With the sea green sea

RUNNING OUT OF TROUBLE (1964)

I kept having these particular little thought schemes that kept happening more and more. At first they wouldn't take up too much of my attention and I'd notice them more after they'd happened than at the instant I was involved. Then it came about that all I was having all the time were these particular little thought schemes around one particular theme. I'd be somewhere in a house with several rooms and all I was thinking each time I went into a new room was how each room would be to live in if I were sentenced to life imprisonment. The thought of being sentenced or who was doing the sentencing or why didn't matter at all. All my particular little thought schemes were concerned with was how to survive in this or that particular room with whatever the room had to offer. If the room had a lot to offer like a fireplace I'd start thinking about wood and digging the wood supply and calculating how long it would last before I'd have to forget about wood and the fireplace and go on to something else like family portraits and family seals and crests and coats of arms. I figured that interest in them articles would last only so long and no longer so I'd hunt around for new stuff to dazzle and titillate like ashtrays made out of milk glass and photographs of the Civil War and a glass table with a glass bowl in the middle filled with glass grapes and glass pears. Then I'd start thinking about food and being fed and eating and quickly decided that I should check out the kitchen and see what sort of prison that would make. I'd be fed there at least but then sooner or later I'd run into the same trouble I had with the wood. Running out trouble. Then I began to see that running out trouble was real trouble and it was the kind of trouble I was running up against all the time and that these particular little thought schemes weren't just hypothetical and all. These particular little thought schemes were really involved in trying to work something out that was happening right there at the time they were going on and not just preparing for something to come. So I ran out the front door and onto the lawn which is green and smooth and serene as Pennsylvania and I yell as loud

81

as all get out that I was in real trouble on account of all I had was glass grapes and a short supply of wood and right next door a short, bald, fat, cigar-in-hand gentleman in red leather slippers walks onto the porch and saunters over to my side of the fence and wraps his fat cigar hand around my neck and says to me not to worry 'cause help was on the way and sure enough a pickup truck stops in front of the lawn and a short fat guy with a baseball cap gets out with an armful a wood.

ELECTRIC FOG

O'Neill
Fog
Electric
Light
Jaimie
Morphine
Sea
Fog
Electric
North
East
Coast
Sad
Electric
Night

* * * * * * * * * * * * * * * * * *

BATTLE LACE
Welts
Bleeding loud
From belting
With buckles
And lace
Across her face
She sure smarts now
Kept by compadres
In battle halls
College dorms and
Mounted cannon
On the peak roofs
Scanning football fields
Like movies

Like life copying movies
Like flesh and blood
Still she sticks around
For lack of another place
To go to

THE MOVEMENT OF STOPPING

I'll sit in one place. It could come about from what I've done before. You know, walking along and just coming to a stop somewhere. Just stopping.

Don't you want to go?

Just stopped. Everything drags you down. There's a collection of junk in your throat, in your chest. Your blood hardens up. I'm standing there and a silver Mercedes Benz comes along and stops right beside me for no special reason except that the light is red. I'm stopped. I stare through their window. I see them surrounded in leather. Leather seats, leather roof, leather clothes. If they moved one inch everything would squeak. They haven't moved hardly at all because of the squeaky leather. Their radio's on. James Brown is screaming to go back to school in his leather pants. She lays her hand in his lap. They stare straight out the window. The light turns green but his joint is getting hard and the leather bulges up. She sees me and smiles. She squeezes his prick. He turns the channel. Little Stevie Wonder is singing about a place in the sun. A guy starts wiping their window with a bloody rag. He grabs the gear shift and rubs up and down. The light changes red. This is really happening. I could go somewhere else.

Why don't you?

I move down the block and begin to stop again. Again I'm stopped. I'm standing there and thinking all about High School. The movement of High School. A cement slab on the Mojave Desert which is architecturally magnificent. A place to bake your feet. A block with circles and incest in the faculty. A little teacher with a baby face getting sucked by the Fine Arts lady. I'm moving out in the world. Look at me move Ma.

Why don't you move?

ROLLING RENAULT

Teddy? Well I can tell you when it was the last time I saw Teddy. He was driving a nineteen-fifty-one green Renault at the time and came by to pick me up. I'd been waiting underneath a billboard sign advertising Ford when he slid into it and I got in. Right away I realized the slide was something peculiar to Teddy's usual method of handling Renaults and I began to question his technique when lo and behold I see a brown paper bag on the back seat and ask him what it's about. Teddy tells me to see for myself and I reach my hand back there and peek in the bag and lo and behold I catch sight of more dexedrine and bennies than I ever saw in my life. Well I turn slowly around and don't say a word. We've been driving for some while now when I notice Teddy ain't stopping for a thing. I begin talking to him, hoping that speaking will bring him down some. I ask him what he's stolen lately at the factory and he tells me it's not a factory but a specialized corporation with branches around the world. I ask him then how he's feeling lately about his job and he asks me how I would feel if I made invisible circuits for future installation in a bigger camera to film the nose cone of Gemini 7 as it turns back toward earth. I see he's in another world and I'm about to turn on WABC when Teddy sees about four miles up the road a nineteen-forty-eight Chrysler sedan slowly pulling across the road. He whips the wheel to the left and the left front wheel hits the curb and the axle breaks and the car hits a lamp post and flips over and rolls four times landing right side up in a gas station with the top crushed and all the glass smashed except for the front window which popped out somewhere on the grass.

THE ESCAPES OF BUSTER KEATON

If you ever have a mind to, what you can do some time instead of what you usually do is turn on the old T.V. and turn down the sound so you can't hear the words and just watch the funny picture. You could also do the reverse of that and turn on the old T.V. and fuck up the picture so it's not a picture and only waves and dots and lights moving up and down and in and out and turn the sound way up. Then you can take part in narrating an escape. If you notice the escapes of Buster Keaton you're bound to learn something. You learn first of all that you don't have to try. You see him in action and you notice it's a double action with two opposites happening simultaneously. You notice the face just being a face and nothing more or less than a face and for that reason it becomes more of a face but don't worry. You notice the body performing more things than a body can perform and being sometimes more than a body and sometimes less and for that reason becoming something more than a body. You see the face not worried about the body and the body not worried about the face and then he escapes. You're trapped watching while he escapes. The thing that strikes you most is that he doesn't worry about being caught.

VOICES FROM THE DEAD

(Monologues written for The Open Theatre 1969)

COWBOY: The Rodeo Association made the Suicide Grip illegal in somethin' like 1959 but that didn't stop no bull rider I knew from usin' the damn thing. First off you take the glove on your grip hand and pull the fingers loose by about three quarters of an inch and wrap them around the rigging so it's like the glove is tied down with your hand stuck inside. Then you pound yer fist shut on the rope with yer free hand 'til you stop the blood from runnin'. When that chute opens boy you hang on like epoxy to wood. This bull I drew was called The Twister and boy he did just that. Circles. Like he was dancin' on a dime. Didn't even have time to mark him once before he had me up against the fence. Never knew eight seconds could be so long. A cowboy knows when he's got a good ride. Soon as he comes out he knows. If it's good he don't even listen for no bell he just rides. If it's good everything's in one place. You just flap with the bucks like you was an extra piece a skin on that bull's back. If it's bad he's got you all crooked and prayin' for balance. Achin' for the bell. This time I knew I was hurtin'. He kept slammin' my legs up against that damn fence and each time I heard a board crack I heard a bone to go along with it. I saw the whole arena zig zagging like a roller coaster ride. The ten gallon hats and American flags. That bullhorn squawkin' about Levis and popcorn and ferris wheels and "Here comes Billie Joe Brody from Thunder Creek, South Dakota on The Twister! Look at this boy ride. Watch out there! Watch out Billie Joe!" Then he had me sideways. My whole body snapped clean across his back. All except that hand. That grip hand stuck in there for dear life. First thing I thought was, "Now they know I'm a cheater. Now they know. They can all see my glove stuck underneath that riggin' rope. Coast to coast T.V. Mom and Pop back in Thunder Creek. Down at the bar. Only T.V. in the whole damn town. Now they know." I felt it come loose at the shoulder. Right where the ball fits into the socket. A cowboy

88

gets to know about anatomy after all them years. Nothin' but flesh and muscle holdin' me onto that bull now. He keeps whippin' me around like a dish towel or somethin'. Slam into that fence. Slam! Somethin' breaks loose. All blood and strings comin' out. All I want is to be free a them hooves. Down he comes straight on my back. Everything breaks. I can feel it. Like my whole insides is made a glass. Everything splinters and shatters. I see the face a the clown. He's got a terror mask on. Usually calm and cool as you please. Now he's wavin' that bandana like an old fish wife chasin' off the neighbors' kids. That bull don't move from me once. Not one inch. He's mad. Mad at me. Mad as all hell and he ain't lettin' me go. Not never. He's got me this time and he knows it. I ain't never gonna get up again. He's makin' me part a the earth. Mashin' me down. Pulverizin' my flesh. Sendin' me back where I come from. Then he's gone. Straight at the crowd, all screamin' and yellin'. Half fear, half ecstasy. They got more than a buck's worth this time out. The gates open on the far end of the arena and I can see this Cadillac comin'. A big black car. Can't tell if it's a hearse or an ambulance. Don't much give a damn. The ground tastes like earth.

STONE MAN: I'm stone. "The Living Stone Man." They call me that. They did. At Pacific Ocean Park. They brought me from Malaysia. They found me like that. Just lying there straight out, stiff. Stiff as a board. "The Living Stiff." Right past the cotton candy machine that spins pink stuff around an aluminum disc. That's where you could have bought a ticket. They have me in a house trailer. The same kind they have on display with butane double burner stoves and fold-out, tuckaway beds. This one has my pictures outside. Black and white snapshots showing me in different positions of stiffness. One where I'm laying straight out horizontal on a chair. Like levitation except there's a chair there. In fact they sometimes display me that way. Only my eyes move.

That's how they know I'm alive. They feed me with a tube. Milk, soup, egg yolks, stuff like that. They hand out hat pins at the door of the trailer for anyone who doesn't believe that I'm really the "Petrified Man." They stick me sometimes but most of the time they get too afraid. They see my eyes moving, looking at them. They get too afraid. One day my eyes stopped moving but they kept me on display anyway. They kept sticking me with needles. In fact more people stuck me with needles now because my eyes stopped moving. I could still feel the needles even though my eyes stopped.

TELEPORTED MAN: I was trying to get to China. My atoms were to be decomposed in New York and recomposed in Hong Kong. They said there was nothing to fear. It had worked hundreds of times before without an accident. I'd saved for five years for this trip. Five years. They had me take off my clothes and enter the tube. I had to lie straight out horizontal with my head up, strapped into the electronic beamer. My legs and arms strapped, my back rigid. I looked straight ahead to the end of the tube or what seemed to be the end. A spiral of light going out and out. Yellow light like the halos you see on Jesus in all the paintings. The sides of the tube glistened and shined, sending off waves of light, like steam heat except it was light. A sound traveled down the tube from the top to the bottom. A line of green light. I'd never seen sound before. It weaved and bobbed as though it were looking for me, like a thin green snake with its tongue spitting. It found me. The top of my head then right in the center of my forehead, like a third eye burrowing in. It felt like an eye at least. A new sight. I could see with my brain. My whole head lit up with the sound. My body became the sound. Pulsing to the vibrations. All the way down my spine and into my rectum. I could feel myself going away. The body. I didn't look down to see because I wasn't afraid. I knew it would work. The epidermis, the tissue, the muscle fibre, the veins,

90

and blood, the bones, the heart, intestines. Each piece growing away from me until there I was, left alone. Hanging in mid air like a ghost. Just my spirit, my brain, no not my brain but something that knew I was there even though I wasn't, in the flesh. I started to move up the tube. Moving through space in a vacuum. Something seemed to pull me along. I was shot out the tube and into space. I could see boats pulling away from the harbor and planes taking off. I was moving at a tremendous rate. I never felt so light and free. Like I was part of the air. Lighter than air. Land vanished and everything below me was water then clouds then high above. I couldn't tell how fast I was going now. Everything seemed timeless and space opened out and out. I'd never felt so free in my life. Then suddenly I couldn't get back. I couldn't go on and I couldn't go back. I knew I was lost. I reached out for my body, for something hard and real. My legs, my arms. Anything. The panic filled me. I was going to die in mid air. Out of my body. Somewhere in space between New York and Hong Kong. I was being pulled toward the stars. Deeper and deeper in space. I searched for my voice but nothing was there. I tried to scream and nothing came out. No one was there to hear me or see me. I was absolutely alone. I longed to be human again. To crash to the earth and die like a man.

HOW LONELY CAN IT GET IN A HOLE?

The bottom fell out. There was no way up to the top. Even the light at the top was black. An endless pit. Stork Clark heard the cars roar by and asked the little boy holding his hand and leading the way, "Why don't they turn their lights on. They can see I'm out here." The little boy didn't answer, afraid to embarrass his blindness. "How lonely can it get in a hole?" the little boy asked. Stork Clark didn't answer. He was driving a team of horses through the timber with a load of coffee for the lumberjacks. "I'm not afraid of the dark," the little boy said. "Well you oughta be," said Stork. All through the village they whispered, "Poor old devil." A silent whisper which Stork understood to be night. "Maybe it's an eclipse. I've seen it get like this up in the Yukon." The boy didn't understand the word "eclipse" but took it to mean a circle. "We've been walking straight North."

"I know my way around kid. I grew up in these woods. Don't forget that. The sun should be comin' before too long. I've seen it like this in the North." He pulled at the boy's hand and took the lead, straining with his head forward like a draft horse. "You oughta let me lead ya Stork. There's a lot a trucks out tonight." Stork broke to the left and broke loose from the boy's grip, walking straight out into the fields toward the woods. The kid ran after him yelling, "Hey! They want me to bring you back for supper Stork! Hey!" Stork kept walking strong stumbling on old plow ruts and plodding on. The kid kept chasing him, pulling at his arm. Stork growled and shoved him away. "I'll find my way out. You tell 'em that. I'll find my way." "But you're heading straight for the woods!"

Stork slipped between a line of blue spruce trees and disappeared. The boy was afraid to go in after him and afraid to go back to the Rest home and tell them he'd lost the old man. He sat down and listened to the crunching snapping footsteps of Stork fade off and go silent. He cried for a while and looked at the moon. He felt the silent secret night coming in and watched the headlights of lumber trucks shake down the road, far off. He watched all the houses and the lights inside. The difference between the outside and the inside. He imagined all the people sitting inside. Warm. Talking. Reading. Knitting. Smoking. Drinking coffee and tea. He got up and walked back through the field to the road. He flagged down a big truck and climbed aboard. "Where to?" The driver asked. The kid just stared. "How lonely can it get in a hole?" he thought.

Printed January 1973 in Santa Barbara for the
Black Sparrow Press by Noel Young. Design by
Barbara Martin. This edition is limited to
1000 copies in paper wrappers; 200 hardcover
copies numbered & signed by the author;
& 26 copies handbound in boards by Earle Gray,
lettered & signed by the author.

SAM SHEPARD was born November 5, 1943, in Fort Sheradon, Illinois. He has lived in Washington, Iowa, Guam, Michigan, Minnesota, Oklahoma, Wisconsin, South Dakota, Arizona, California, Canada, London, Mexico, and New York City.

His plays include: *Up to Thursday*, Cherry Lane Theatre and Martinique Theatre; *Fourteen Hundred Thousand*, Fire House Theatre and NET Theatre; *The Unseen Hand* and *Forensic and the Navigators*, Astor Place Theatre; *La Turista*, American Place Theatre; *Operation Sidewinder*, Lincoln Center; *Cowboys #2*, Mark Taper Forum; *Back Bog Beast Bait* and *The Cowboy Mouth*, American Place Theatre; *Mad Dog Blues*, Theatre Genesis; *Shaved Splits* and *Melodrama Play*, La Mama Theatre; *The Tooth of Crime*, Open Space Theatre.

He has also written two films: *Zabriskie Point* (Antonioni) and *Me and My Brother* (Robert Frank).

Hawk Moon is his first published book.